THE STORY OF ALEXANDER HAMILTON

A Biography Book for New Readers

Written by
Christine Platt

Illustrated by
Raquel Martín

ROCKRIDGE PRESS

For Lin-Manuel Miranda. Thank you for creating a musical that my daughter, Nalah Palmer, sang "Non-Stop!"

For general information on our other products and services or to obtain technical support, please contact our Customer Care Department within the United States at (866) 744-2665, or outside the United States at (510) 253-0500.

Rockridge Press publishes its books in a variety of electronic and print formats. Some content that appears in print may not be available in electronic books, and vice versa.

Interior and Cover Designer: Stephanie Sumulong
Art Producer: Hillary Frileck
Editor: Orli Zuravicky
Production Editor: Ruth Sakata Corley

Illustration © Raquel Martín, pp. iv, 3, 4, 6, 9, 12, 13, 15, 16, 19, 20, 21, 23, 26, 28, 32, 35, 37, 39, 42, 44; Shutterstock p 47; Istock pp. 49, 50. Author photo courtesy of © Nora E. Jones Photography. Illustrator photo courtesy of © Laura Mariel Nellar.

ISBN: Print 978-1-64611-425-2 | eBook 978-1-64611-426-9

R1

Printed in China

TABLE OF CONTENTS

CHAPTER 1

A FOUNDING FATHER IS BORN

★ Meet Alexander Hamilton ★

Alexander Hamilton was born on a small Caribbean island called Nevis. As a boy, he loved to read. He also liked to play tricks on people. Those who knew him couldn't have imagined that the young troublemaker would one day grow up to be one of America's **Founding Fathers** and help form the **government**. Surely Alexander never thought his face would one day be on a ten-dollar bill!

Alexander grew from a playful child to an **orphan** teenager to an important man in America's history. He had to learn how to take care of himself at a young age. He worked hard and learned to write well—both skills later helped him get to America.

From the moment Alexander arrived in New York, he spent his life helping write fair laws and fighting for what he believed in: creating

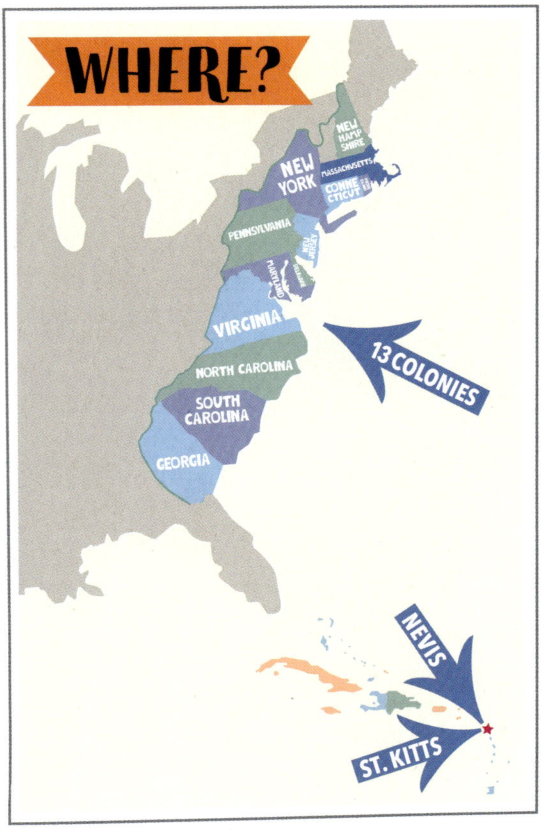

a new nation led by honest men. Though Alexander had a difficult childhood, and it didn't seem likely that he would grow up to do great things, he found a way to do just that!

★ Hamilton's World ★

Alexander Hamilton was born around January 11 in either 1755 or 1757. (His exact birthdate is not known.) His parents were Rachel Faucette Lavien and James Hamilton.

During Alexander's childhood, two big countries called Britain and France were trying to grow richer by **colonizing** North America and South America. Britain ruled over the Caribbean island of Nevis where Alexander grew up. It also owned an area of land in America that was known as the **Thirteen Colonies**.

JUMP IN THE THINK TANK

What do you think are some of the best things about living on a Caribbean island? What would be some of the hardest?

Britain and France began battling each other for control of the Americas in 1756. This war lasted seven years. For much of Alexander's childhood, British people living in the Thirteen Colonies and the Caribbean struggled to survive.

Although Nevis was beautiful, life on the island could be difficult. The war hurt the island's **economy**. Also, few crops could grow there. Those that could were sometimes destroyed by bad weather or plant sickness, so there was often not enough food. Alexander's family was fairly **wealthy**, so he and his brother, James Jr., didn't have as hard a time as others.

Many European settlers on Nevis **enslaved** Africans and made them work on their sugar **plantations**. The work was very hard. Sometimes fights broke out between the **plantation** owners and enslaved Africans who wanted to escape.

Alexander thought **slavery** was unfair. He did not like the way slaves on Nevis were treated.

MYTH & FACT

MYTH: Europeans had always lived on the island of Nevis.

FACT: Europeans were not the original people of any Caribbean island. People from Britain, France, Spain, and other countries came to the Caribbean in search of goods and resources.

Though Alexander grew up on a small island, he knew he was born to do great things. Little did Alexander know that Britain's rule over America would play a big role in his future.

WHEN?

1753 — James Hamilton, Alexander's older brother, is born.

1755/57 — Alexander Hamilton is born.

CHAPTER 2
THE EARLY YEARS

Growing Up in the Caribbean Islands

Alexander's mother, Rachel, was born to a fairly wealthy family on Nevis. She married Johann Michael Lavien, whom she believed was also wealthy. They had a son named Peter. Soon after, Rachel found out that Johann was not only a poor man, but a mean man. Rachel was so unhappy she decided to leave her family.

In the 1700s, most women did not leave their husbands, so Rachel knew people would not understand. She also knew she wouldn't be allowed to marry again. Still, when Rachel met James Hamilton, a Scottish **merchant**, they fell in love. Although they were not married, Rachel and James lived together and had two sons, James Jr. and Alexander. They raised the boys in their family home.

Alexander and his brother had lots of books, played on sandy beaches, and climbed palm trees. Still, in the 1700s, having a child out of **wedlock** was not generally accepted. Other children would tease Alexander and his brother. They were probably not allowed to go to the local schools, which were owned by the Church of

Hamilton Family Tree

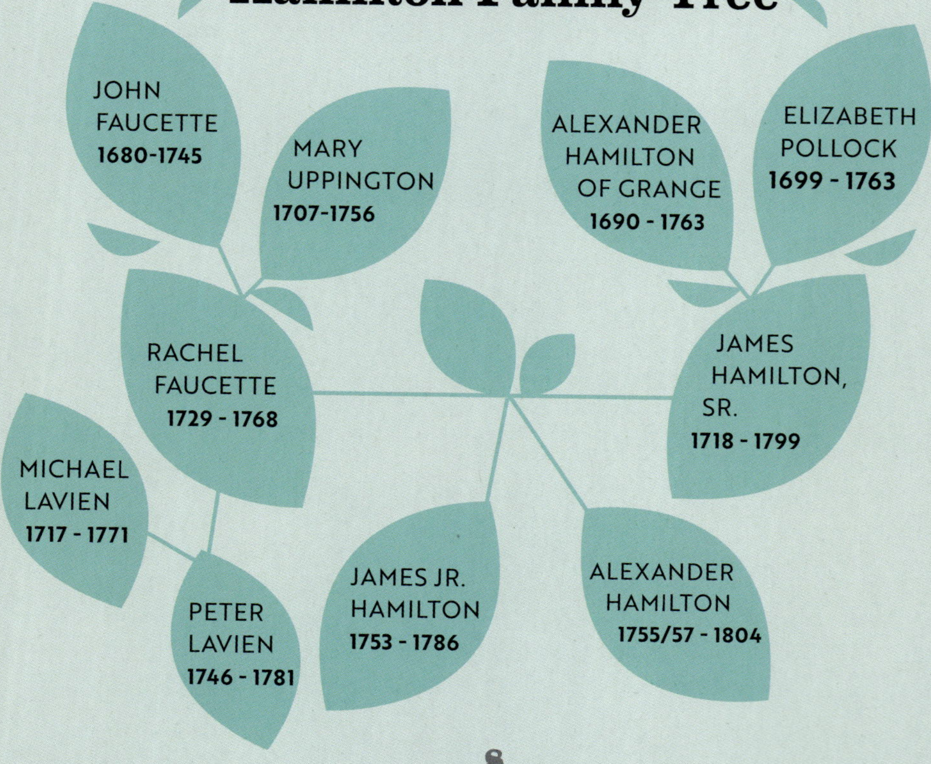

England, so the boys were tutored. Alexander loved writing and learning as much as he could. One of his favorite subjects was English, especially poetry.

Alexander's childhood was mostly good. Soon, though, this would change.

★ From Island to Immigrant ★

In 1765, when Alexander was about 10, his family moved to an island called St. Croix. Soon afterward, Alexander's father decided not to live with them anymore. Alexander's mother found a house for her small family. She opened a store on the first floor. The family lived upstairs.

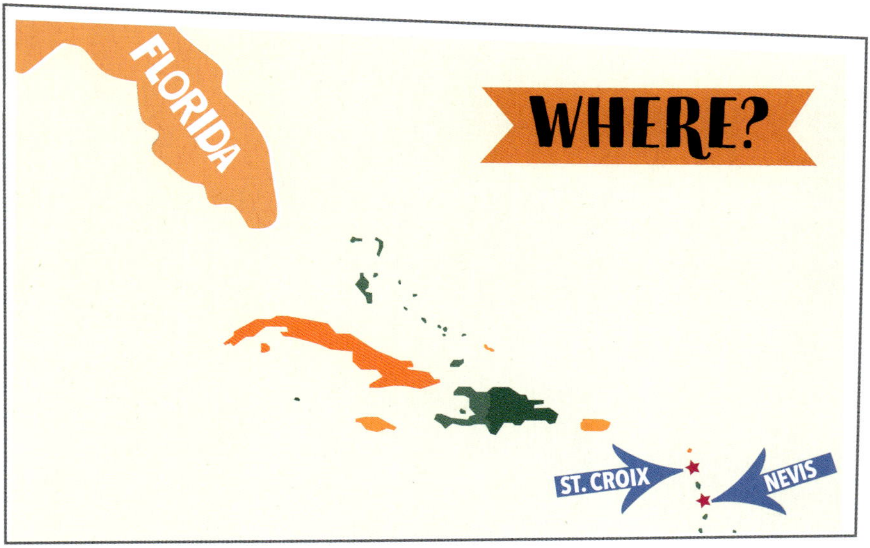

That year, Alexander and his mother got yellow fever, a terrible illness that causes high fevers and a lot of pain. Though Alexander got better, his mother sadly passed away.

Alexander and James Jr. went to live with a cousin named Peter Lytton. To help pay bills, Alexander went to work for a merchant named Nicholas Cruger. The name of his company was

Beekman and Cruger, and it sold and traded mostly clothing and food. Sometimes, though, they handled shipments of Africans to sell them into slavery. Alexander didn't like seeing people enslaved. Still, his job was to help the process run smoothly.

Several months later, Peter died. The two brothers had to be separated. James Jr. went to work with a local **carpenter**. Alexander kept working for Beekman and Cruger, but was adopted by a man named Thomas Stevens.

JUMP IN THE THINK TANK

Alexander lost several family members when he was young. How do you think he felt being separated from his brother, James Jr., too?

MYTH & FACT

MYTH: Enslaved Africans were treated well and did not suffer.

FACT: European plantation owners often treated enslaved Africans very badly and abused them. Alexander thought this was unfair.

Four years later, in 1772, a terrible hurricane hit St. Croix. Alexander wrote a letter about it, which the local newspaper soon **published**. Because his writing was so good, people came together to help send him away to school. Soon, Alexander was on a ship to America!

WHEN?

1765	1768	1772
The Hamiltons move to St. Croix.	Rachel dies; Alexander and James Jr. are separated.	A hurricane hits St. Croix; Alexander goes to America.

CHAPTER 3

WELCOME TO AMERICA

★ A Dream Comes to Life ★

In October 1772, Alexander arrived in Boston Harbor. By the fall of 1773, Alexander traveled to New York City to attend King's College (known today as Columbia University). New York was one of the thirteen colonies owned by Britain. The British made the colonists pay high **taxes**. This made it hard for them to buy even basic food and supplies. There were some colonists, known as

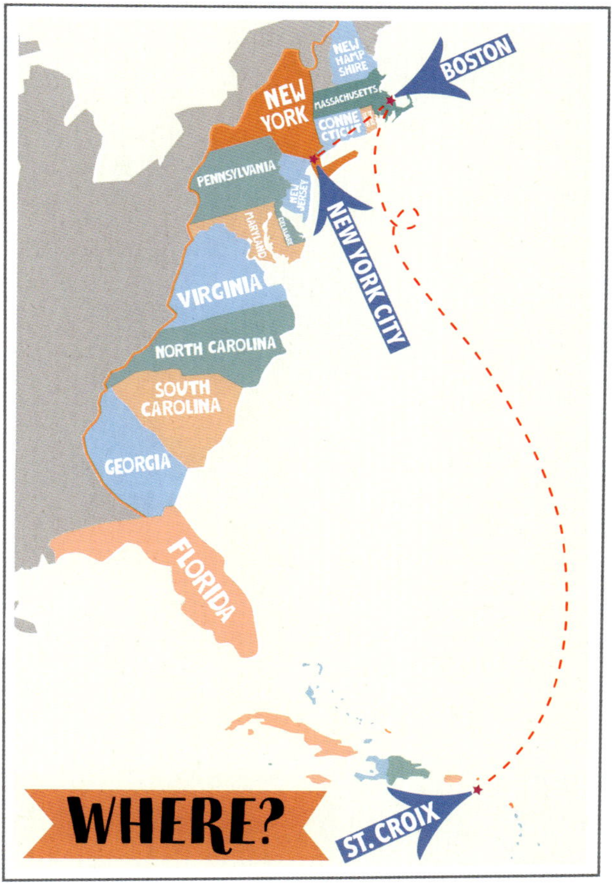

patriots, who wanted America to separate from British rule. They knew they might have to go to war to become **independent**, or separate. There were also some colonists, known as loyalists, who did not want to separate from Britain. As time went on, more and more people became patriots. They began planning a **revolution**, or fight, to gain their independence.

> “I wish there was a war.”

On December 16, 1773, several patriots in Boston went on board ships filled with tea the

British wanted to sell. The patriots threw most of the tea into the water. This **protest** is known as the Boston Tea Party.

Alexander sided with the patriots. He joined in talks and wrote **anonymous** articles explaining why people should join the patriots. Secretly, Alexander wanted the countries to go to war. He believed in America's independence. He also thought being a soldier could help him succeed in life.

Even with the talk of revolution, Alexander studied hard at King's College. He knew having a college degree could also help him succeed.

Many college students were from wealthy families. As a poor orphan, Alexander sometimes felt like everyone was better than he was. Still, he kept studying. Alexander even made a few friends, like Hercules Mulligan, the Marquis de Lafayette, and Aaron Burr. Later on, one of these men would become Alexander's biggest enemy.

JUMP —IN THE— THINK TANK

If you lived in the colonies during the American Revolution, would you have been a patriot or loyalist? Why?

★ Seeds of Revolution ★

In 1775, Alexander and other students at King's College formed a **militia** called Hearts of Oak in case there was a revolution. They wore short green jackets pinned with red tin hearts that said "God and Our Right" and round leather hats with the words "Liberty or Death" on the front. In April 1775, Alexander's wish for a war came true. The first official battles of the **American Revolution**, also called the Revolutionary War, took place in Massachusetts, at Lexington and Concord.

Though Alexander sided with the patriots and wanted to fight Britain, he did not want to fight with loyalists in America. On May 10, 1775, an angry crowd gathered to attack a well-known loyalist, Myles Cooper, who was the president of Alexander's college. Alexander stopped the crowd by giving a speech, and Mr. Cooper was able to escape.

Alexander became known as a gifted speaker and writer. His public speeches and writings about the revolution made many people want to join the patriots, and helped move America toward independence.

In order to fight the British, the colonists would need to have a big army. On June 15, 1775, George Washington was put in charge of the **Continental Army**. In August 1775, the Hearts

of Oak helped steal and hide several British **cannons**. Because the militia's members had been so brave, they were chosen to be a part of the Continental Army. Alexander became captain of artillery with its tanks and large guns. This was just the beginning of Alexander's time in the military.

WHEN?

1772	1773	1775
Alexander arrives in Boston.	Patriots destroy tea at Boston Harbor.	The militia from King's College steals British cannons.

CHAPTER 4

REVOLUTION!

★ General Washington's Aide ★

When Alexander spoke about independence, he often made people believe that America should be free from British control. Helping people see the importance of the Revolutionary War meant he could also get other men to agree to be soldiers.

Senior officers in the Continental Army saw that people listened to Alexander. Because of this, several officers wanted Alexander to be their personal assistant. One very important person was also watching Alexander: General George Washington. Many men may have jumped at the chance to serve as General Washington's assistant, but Alexander did not.

JUMP —IN THE— THINK TANK

Why do you think it was so hard for Alexander to leave the battlefield and work for General Washington? Hint: Remember how men gained honor during this time.

He really enjoyed fighting on the battlefield and was proud to be a soldier. Working for Washington would take him away from the fighting. Still, it was such a great opportunity that Alexander agreed to work for General Washington starting March 1, 1777, when he was around 20 years old.

As one of General Washington's right-hand men, Alexander had a lot to do. In the 1700s, the only ways to talk to someone were in person or by writing letters. Alexander's job was to write to senior officers and people in the Continental Congress, the government of the Thirteen Colonies. He would give the latest news and ask for whatever was needed. He also went to meetings that General Washington couldn't attend.

Love and War

Despite his work with George Washington, Alexander still found time for fun. He liked to go to parties, dance, and talk with others. He was handsome and many women had crushes on him. Though he loved being admired, Alexander wasn't thinking about marriage. This all changed in the winter of 1780 when he saw Elizabeth "Eliza" Schuyler at a big winter ball in Morristown, New Jersey.

Alexander and Eliza quickly fell in love. Though Alexander wasn't wealthy, Eliza's father agreed to their marriage. On December 14, 1780, Alexander and Eliza had a wedding at the Schuyler mansion.

MYTH & FACT

MYTH: During the time of the American Revolution, only men were wealthy.

FACT: A man's wealth was based on what his family owned, such as land and businesses. The same was true for women like Eliza Schuyler and her two sisters.

In early 1781, Alexander decided to stop working for General Washington so he could be a soldier again. While Alexander was away, Eliza lived with her family in Albany, New York. But Alexander visited her often. He loved talking to her about what would happen if the Continental Army won the war. America would be a new

country! Leaders would have to figure out the best ways to govern the land and people.

In the summer of 1781, Alexander was sent to a battle in Yorktown, Virginia. A few months later, Alexander received more exciting news: Eliza was pregnant with their first child.

WHEN?

The Colonies declare independence.

1776

Alexander and Eliza Schuyler fall in love and marry.

1780

Alexander is sent to battle; Eliza learns she is pregnant.

1781

CHAPTER 5
HAMILTON THE WAR HERO

Battle of Yorktown

Since he was a young boy, Alexander had wanted to lead men into battle. On September 28, 1781, his dream came true. Along with General Washington, Alexander joined almost 17,000 French and Continental soldiers to fight the British in Yorktown.

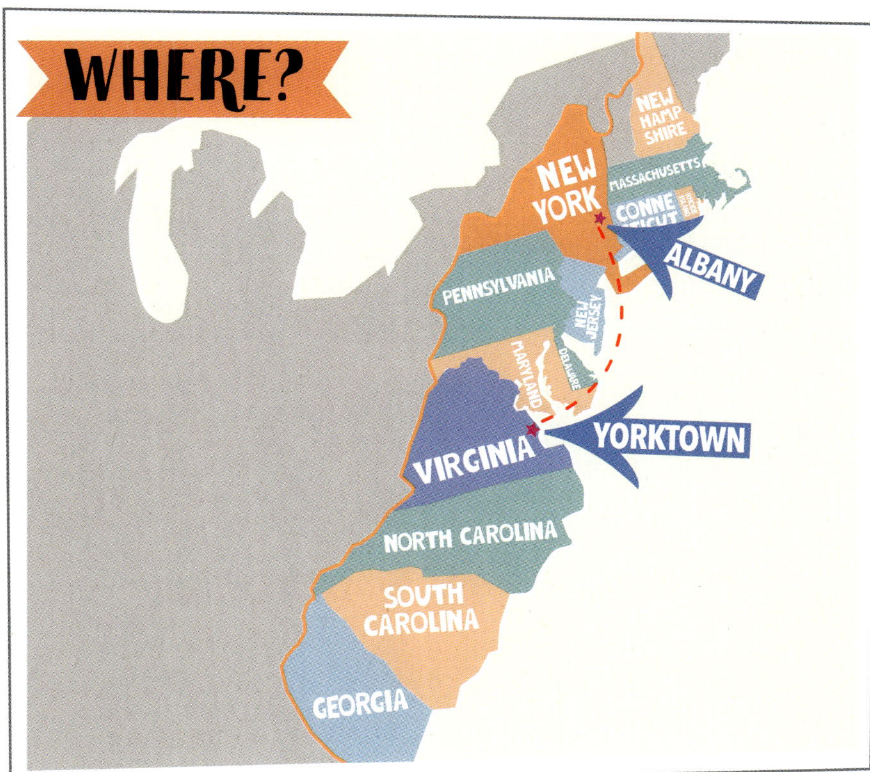

JUMP IN THE THINK TANK

Why do you think Alexander wanted to fight in the Revolutionary War so badly? What do you think he hoped to do?

October 14, 1781 was a moonless night. The fields in Yorktown were very dark. Alexander got an idea—what if the Continental soldiers surprised the British with a nighttime attack? Alexander's troops didn't use guns, only **bayonets**, or large blades, so they could move quietly. The British troops had no idea they were being surrounded. Within ten minutes, Alexander and his troops forced the British to surrender and helped win the war!

The battle of Yorktown lasted from September 28 to October 17, 1781. It ended up being the last major land battle in the Revolutionary War. Newspapers around the country published the story of Alexander's victory. Of course, Alexander was proud of himself. He'd finally been recognized as a great soldier and leader.

★ A Political Future ★

During the Battle of Yorktown, Alexander missed Eliza very much. He wrote to her a lot and hoped to return home in time for their first child's birth—and he did! In January 1782, their first son, Philip, was born.

Alexander loved being a father. He decided not to be in the military anymore so he could spend more time with his family. Eager to set himself up with a good job, he chose to become a **lawyer**. When Alexander wasn't spending time with Eliza and Philip, he was studying. With the end of the Revolutionary War, Alexander wanted to help build the new nation of America.

While studying to be a lawyer, Alexander was asked to be the tax collector for New York. It was a job similar to the one he'd had as a kid with Mr. Cruger. Unlike the taxes that Britain made the colonists pay, the taxes set up in America were created to be fair. But it was very difficult. Collecting taxes made Alexander realize that America would need a really good system for its money, now that it was an independent nation.

> "I have thought it **my duty** to exhibit things **as they are, not** as they ought to be."

Once students are done with law school, they have to pass a hard test called the bar exam before they can be lawyers. Alexander studied a lot for the bar exam, and he passed!

In 1783, Alexander moved his small family to New York City and opened his law office. Another man, whom Hamilton had known for years, also opened a law office in New York on the very same street as Hamilton—Aaron Burr. Both men were excited to work in **politics**. Though friends, they had always competed against one another in a playful sort of way. Little did Alexander know that one day soon, they would become enemies.

Philip Hamilton is born.

1782

Alexander passes the bar exam; opens law office in NYC.

1783

WHEN?

CHAPTER 6

THE NEW NATION

Serving the Continental Congress

Before and during the Revolutionary War, the Continental Congress governed the Thirteen Colonies. With independence, the new nation followed a new set of rules and laws called the Articles of Confederation. People had different ideas about these rules.

MYTH & **FACT**

Myth: America always had a president, even during the Revolutionary War.

Fact: George Washington was elected to serve as America's first president in 1789!

In 1782, Alexander was chosen to be part of the new government, called the Confederation Congress, of the now independent nation.

Alexander believed the new nation should have a strong government with strong new rules and an army for protection. Along with two other leaders, John Jay and James Madison, Alexander helped write some new articles, which are like rules—Alexander wrote 51 of the 85 new articles. He also wrote **essays** explaining why these new rules were needed.

These articles and essays were published in the newspapers and are known as the Federalist Papers. Soon, leaders from different states began talking about creating a new set of rules altogether called a constitution.

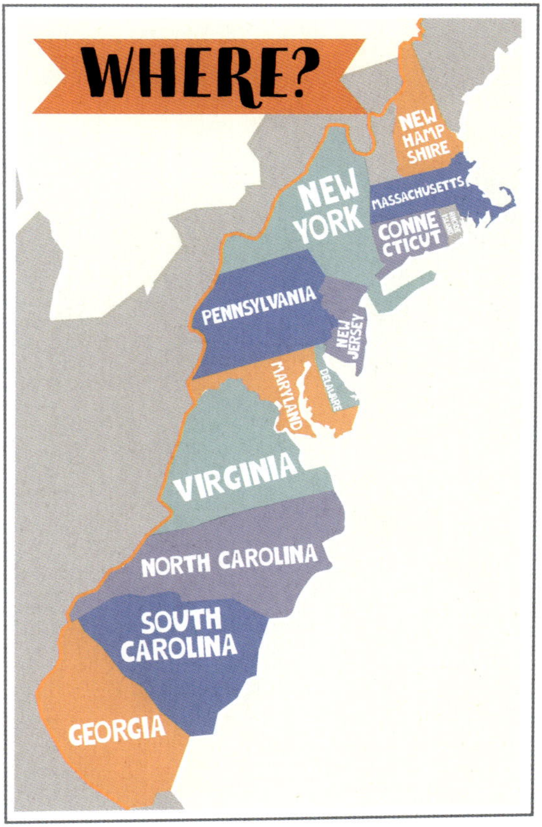

From May 25 to September 17, 1787, 55 leaders came together for a meeting known as the Constitutional Convention. They came from the new states of Connecticut, Delaware, Georgia, Maryland, Massachusetts, New Hampshire, New Jersey, New York, North Carolina, Pennsylvania, South Carolina, and Virginia. The 55 men are known as the Framers of the Constitution.

Of course, Alexander was among them. In September 1787, the Framers of the Constitution

came to an agreement. The new nation's constitution became law on June 21, 1788. On March 4, 1789, the nation had a new government.

★ Secretary of the Treasury ★

New York City was the first capital of the United States. There, George Washington became the nation's first president on April 30, 1789. Under the new government, there were many jobs to do. Alexander was asked to be secretary of the treasury. That meant he would decide how the United States set up its money systems. Still, like before, some people disagreed with Alexander's ideas.

One of Alexander's biggest ideas was to pay back state **debt**, or the money that the states of the new nation owed because of the war. Alexander's plan to pay off state debt was to create one bank with its own money, or **currency**, for the whole nation. Many people

disagreed with this idea. They were afraid a national bank would only help wealthy people. Even so, President Washington believed in Alexander. With his and others' support, Alexander got Congress to agree to form the nation's first bank. The United States still follows many of Alexander's ideas about money to this day!

While many people were happy for Alexander's success, others were very jealous that Alexander got so much praise. Aaron Burr was especially upset that Alexander was so

JUMP -IN THE- THINK TANK

Why do you think men like Aaron Burr disliked men like Alexander?

well-liked by George Washington, was able to get so much done, and had become a strong leader. Soon, Alexander could no longer trust Aaron Burr. What was once a friendship took a turn for the worse, and Alexander decided Aaron Burr was no longer his friend.

WHEN?

1787	1788	1789	1791
Alexander helps write the Federalist Papers.	The new constitution becomes law.	Alexander becomes secretary of the treasury.	Alexander establishes the nation's first bank and currency.

CHAPTER 7

FINANCIAL FOUNDING FATHER

★ Family Life ★

It was hard for Alexander to be away from his growing family. He now had five children—Philip, Angelica, Alexander, James, and John. In 1795, Alexander left his job to spend more time with his family.

> "Who talks most about freedom and equality? Is it not those who hold the bill of rights in one hand and a whip for [frightened] slaves in the other?"

Alexander never forgot the enslaved people he saw as a boy. As an adult, he spoke out against slavery and in favor of the need for freedom. He believed everyone should be treated respectfully.

Throughout his life, people often disagreed with Alexander. Though he wasn't bothered by this, Philip, his oldest son, often stood up for him. In the summer of 1801, a lawyer named George Eacker spoke badly about Alexander. Philip wanted George to apologize. When George refused, Philip challenged him to a **duel**.

In the 1700s and early 1800s, when men disagreed and couldn't solve the problem by talking, they would duel using guns. A duel had rules. The men would walk ten steps away from each other, turn, and fire. Most of the time, no one was actually killed. Usually, both men would fire their guns in the air to show the end of the disagreement.

On November 22, 1801, in Weehawken, New Jersey, Philip got ready for his first duel. He followed his father's advice—after walking ten steps, he turned and shot his gun into the air. George Eacker did not. Instead, he chose to shoot Philip. Sadly, Philip died shortly thereafter.

JUMP
-IN THE-
THINK
TANK

How do you think Alexander felt after Philip's death? Do you think he wished he hadn't told his son to make the right choice?

Alexander was deeply upset by Philip's death. A few years later, though, Alexander would find himself at his own duel. With whom? Aaron Burr, of course.

The Final Duel

Over time, Alexander and Aaron Burr's dislike for each other grew. In 1801, Aaron Burr became the nation's vice president under President Thomas Jefferson. Alexander did not agree with many of Burr's ideas and told some people about his feelings. What Alexander said about Aaron

Burr got published in a newspaper. When Burr read it, he thought what Alexander said about him hurt his chances for success in politics—and he was furious!

Vice President Burr wanted an explanation and demanded Alexander apologize. When Alexander refused, Burr challenged him to a duel. In the early morning hours of July 11, 1804, Alexander showed up in Weehawken, New Jersey, to duel Burr.

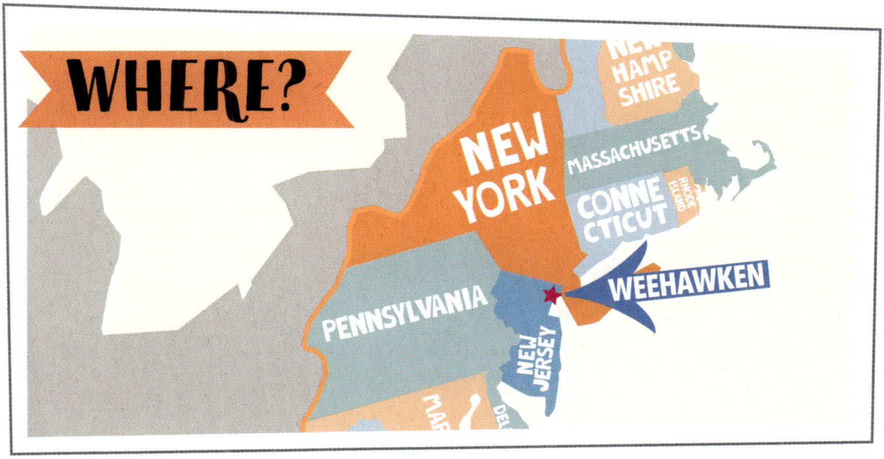

Both men walked ten steps before turning and firing their weapons. Alexander raised his gun and shot into the air. But Vice President Burr

shot and wounded Alexander. Alexander died the following day. He didn't live to see his 50th birthday.

Despite his untimely death, Alexander Hamilton is considered one of America's great Founding Fathers. From the work he did during the Revolutionary War to setting up the nation's first bank and currency, Alexander Hamilton helped make America the strong country it is today. He dedicated his life to leading and fighting for what he believed in.

Sadly, Alexander Hamilton is the one Founding Father who didn't live to see many of the benefits of his work. Still, he lives on in history books and even on stage through the award-winning musical *Hamilton*. And, of course, millions of people see Alexander Hamilton's face every day—all they have to do is look at a ten-dollar bill.

WHEN?

1795	1801	1804	1804
Alexander leaves his government job.	Philip is killed in a duel with George Eacker in November.	Aaron Burr shoots Alexander in a duel on July 11.	Alexander Hamilton dies on July 12.

CHAPTER 8

SO...WHO WAS ALEXANDER HAMILTON?

★ Challenge Accepted! ★

Now that you have learned all about Alexander's amazing life as a leader in the Revolutionary War and one of America's Founding Fathers, let's test your new knowledge in a little who, what, when, where, why, and how quiz. Feel free to look back in the text to find the answers if you need to, but try to remember first!

1 Where was Alexander born?

→ A On the island of St. Kitts

→ B On the island of St. Croix

→ C On the island of Nevis

→ D In New York City

2 What was Alexander's older brother's name?

→ A James Jr.

→ B Alexander III

→ C Philip

→ D George

3 What job did Alexander's first boss, Mr. Cruger, do?

- → A Lawyer
- → B Tax collector
- → C Doctor
- → D Merchant

4 How did Alexander's mother die?

- → A Yellow fever
- → B Scarlet fever
- → C Pneumonia
- → D Influenza

5 What type of natural disaster struck the island of St. Croix and changed the course of Alexander's life?

- → A An earthquake
- → B A hurricane
- → C A tsunami
- → D An avalanche

6 **What was the name of the first college Alexander attended?**

- → A Queen's College
- → B Princeton College
- → C Boston University
- → D King's College

7 **Before the Revolutionary War began, Alexander formed a group with his fellow classmates. What was the name of the group?**

- → A The Hearts of Oak
- → B The Green Oaks
- → C The Stars of Oak
- → D The Patriots of Oak

8 **Where did Alexander meet Elizabeth "Eliza" Schuyler? At a winter ball in:**

- → A New York
- → B Virginia
- → C New Jersey
- → D St. Croix

9 **What was the name of the last land battle of the Revolutionary War? (Hint: It was where Alexander had a big victory!)**

→ A The Battle of New York City
→ B The Battle at Boston Harbor
→ C The Battle of Yorktown
→ D The Battle of Philadelphia

10 **What was the name of Alexander and Eliza's first son?**

→ A Peter
→ B Paul
→ C Pedro
→ D Philip

Answer Key: 1. C; 2. A; 3. D; 4. A; 5. B; 6. D; 7. A; 8. C; 9. C; 10. D

★ Our World ★

How has Alexander's work changed our world today? Let's look at a few things that have happened because of Alexander Hamilton.

→ Alexander Hamilton wrote most of the articles and essays known as the Federalist Papers. Alexander's writings helped convince the other Founding Fathers to create the constitution that America follows today.

→ As the U.S. Department of the Treasury's first secretary, Alexander helped America pay back money it owed after the Revolutionary War. Many of his plans were so careful and important that America still uses them today!

→ Alexander Hamilton spoke of his beliefs that slavery was unfair and cruel. Few people know that in 1785, Alexander helped establish the New York Manumission Society to help end slavery—this was many years before the slavery **abolitionist** movement began in the early 1800s.

JUMP IN THE THINK TANK FOR MORE!

Now let's think a little more about what Alexander Hamilton did, the ways he changed how people viewed independence, and how that affected the world we currently live in.

- → What do you think America would be like if people like Alexander hadn't fought for independence?
- → Alexander had a lot of influence and power. What if he hadn't spoken out against slavery and in favor of the importance of freedom for all people?
- → What if Alexander had never come to America? Can you imagine how different the Constitution might be today?

Glossary

abolitionist: a person who works to end something, especially slavery

American Revolution: colonists' rebellion from 1775 to 1783; also called the Revolutionary War

anonymous: when a person writes something but doesn't use their name

bayonet: a knife at the end of a gun that soldiers use in battle; a weapon

cannon: a large, heavy gun

carpenter: a person who builds things out of wood

colonizing: when people go to a foreign country to claim the land as their own

Continental Army: the organized military for the colonists

currency: a system of money that is used, especially in a country or group of countries

debt: something that is owed or due, usually money

duel: a contest between two people used to settle a disagreement, often with deadly weapons like guns or swords

economy: a country's source of wealth and resources

enslave: to force a person to work without giving them freedom to choose and without paying them for their service

essay: a piece of writing, usually not as long as a book

Founding Fathers: the men who helped create the rules and ideas that formed the United States of America around the time of independence from Britain

government: the office that controls and manages people who live in a particular place

independent: free from the control of another

lawyer: one whose job is to know all about the rules and laws of a government

merchant: buyer and seller of goods

militia: a military group created by civilians

orphan: a young person who has no living parents

plantation: a large piece of land where crops like cotton, tobacco, and sugar are grown and harvested

politics: activities related to governing a city, state, country, or nation

protest: the act of objecting to something

publish: to make a public announcement, usually in a newspaper or other publication

revolution: to fight against the ruling government

slavery: A system of labor that requires people to work against their will and without pay

tax: money the government collects from its citizens to help pay for things that everyone needs, like schools and roads

Thirteen Colonies: The first colonies formed in what would become the United States. The colonies were (in order of formation): New Hampshire, Massachusetts, Connecticut, Rhode Island, New York, New Jersey, Pennsylvania, Delaware, Maryland, Virginia, North Carolina, South Carolina, and Georgia

wealthy: having plenty or being rich

wedlock: the state of being married

Bibliography

Books

Chernow, Ron. *Alexander Hamilton*. New York: Penguin Books, 2004.

Fritz, Jean. *Alexander Hamilton: The Outsider*. New York: Puffin Books, 2011.

Hood, Ann. *Alexander Hamilton: Little Lion*. The Treasure Chest 2. New York: Grosset & Dunlap, 2012.

Kulling, Monica. *Alexander Hamilton: From Orphan to Founding Father*. New York: Random House Young Readers, 2017.

McNamara, Margaret. *Eliza: The Story of Elizabeth Schuyler Hamilton*. New York: Schwartz & Wade, 2018.

Government Sites

Library of Congress—Washington, DC. https://www.loc.gov.

U.S. Department of the Treasury—Washington, DC. https://home.treasury.gov.

Historical Sites

Hamilton House—Charlestown, Nevis, Caribbean

Yorktown Battlefield—Yorktown, Virginia

Hamilton Grange National Memorial—New York City

Alexander Hamilton Grave—Trinity Church, New York City

Schuyler Mansion State Historic Site—Albany, New York

Acknowledgments

The Founding Fathers were faced with the difficult task of creating laws and rules to govern a new nation. Americans remain grateful for their service in developing a constitution that promotes liberty and justice for all.

About the Author

CHRISTINE PLATT is a passionate advocate for social justice and policy reform. She holds a BA in Africana Studies from the University of South Florida, an MA in African and African American Studies from The Ohio State University, and a JD from Stetson University College of Law. Christine is a believer in the power of storytelling as a tool for social change, and her work centers on teaching race, equity, diversity, and inclusion to people of all ages.

About the Illustrator

RAQUEL MARTÍN is a Spanish illustrator from Barcelona based in the beautiful island of Minorca. Her work has appeared in different magazines and she has illustrated several picture books.